University *of* Illinois

Past *&* Present

Urbana-Champaign

UNIVERSITY *of* ILLINOIS
PAST *&* PRESENT
URBANA-CHAMPAIGN

PHOENIX PUBLISHING
URBANA, ILLINOIS

UNIVERSITY OF ILLINOIS ARCHIVES / B A STRA CH POSTCARDS

© 1995 Phoenix Publishing

    Printed on acid-free paper

    Manufactured in the United States of America

ISBN 1-886154-09-0

Phoenix Publishing

    300 West Main Street

    Urbana, Illinois 61801

    U.S.A.

The majority of images in this book have been provided
by the University of Illinois Archives and the Alumni
Association Archives.

We have made every effort to credit both our source
and the photographer for images included. We apologize
for any omissions and welcome corrections, as we plan to
amend future editions.

CONTENTS

5

FOREWORD

Albums, bags, and boxes of photographs can be found in the basements and attics of nearly every house in America. Picnics, graduations, kids on bikes, vacations, weddings, and football in the front yard come back to life in those preserved moments.

Family elders fill in the gaps—the *whos* and the *whens*—for their children and their children's children. The young ones are drawn to the old images: when a horse was the family car, when Grandma was a flapper, when Mom wore pants and worked in the defense plant. Then the photographs go back to the attic and basement, until another holiday visit, a move, or a death prompts us to turn the album pages once more.

The University of Illinois at Urbana-Champaign has an "attic" full of photographs, too. The Illini Family photos, some 87,000 of them, are in the campus archives and library. As with every family's amateur snapshots, there are faces unidentified, dates missing, places vaguely familiar but so changed by time as to be nearly unrecognizable.

Within these pages, you will find a selection of more than 300 black and white and color photographs of people and places connected to the Urbana-Champaign campus. Some photos are historic, others contemporary. *University of Illinois: Past & Present* captures a cross-section of the visible life of this campus. It's an abbreviated family album that condenses the 127-year life of the Urbana-Champaign campus onto fewer than 200 pages.

James Stukel

I first walked this campus in 1962 as a graduate student in mechanical engineering; the University was already 94 years old. I learned to teach and do research on the north campus, now home to a half-dozen new buildings, open spaces, and fountains. My wife, Joan, earned an MBA here. I became a professor and a sometime administrator at Urbana-Champaign. We reared our four children—three are Urbana-Champaign grads—in the shadow of the familiar landmarks of the Illini Union, the Auditorium, and the big Library. In the summer of 1995, I returned to Urbana-Champaign after a decade of exciting work at the University of Illinois at Chicago to become the fifteenth president of the University. My new office is mere steps from the grave of the first regent, John Milton Gregory, who, though brilliant, could not have imagined how the Illini Family would grow and prosper. He would be amazed.

University of Illinois: Past & Present was published with alumni in mind. The Urbana-Champaign campus boasts more that 277,000 graduates who have earned 400,000 degrees. All of those graduates have their own immutable memories of people, places, and events that shaped their campus experiences. The photos that fill these pages may jibe with those memories, or may—because of the passage of time and the transformation of place—be new, never seen, never experienced. The all-female Rifle and Pistol Club of the 1930s is new to this alumnus, but the Illini Union "free speech" plaza that was built to commemorate the campus' centennial is a familiar walkway. I wasn't on campus when Louis Armstrong performed in the 1950s, but I know members of Medicare 7, 8, or 9, who picked up their horns in the '60s and are still going strong as goodwill ambassadors to alumni around the globe. I never saw the campus' old Main Building, called "the Elephant," because my predecessors razed it before I was born. But these, and all of the pictures in this fine book, have meaning to those of us in the Illini Family because they are our shared past, a continuum of people and places that compose our family history.

We are, of course, a restless family. Our fellow alums are scattered across the globe; we are in every profession and industry; we are seldom "home" in Urbana-Champaign. Let *University of Illinois: Past & Present* bring you back in time and place and help you relive what I'm certain were special years.

James J. Stukel MS '63, PhD '68

James J. Stukel MS '63, PhD '68, became President of the University of Illinois in August of 1995, after twenty-seven years of continuous service to the institution. He is only the second alumnus to serve the University as president. Previously, Dr. Stukel was Chancellor of the University's Chicago campus, and he remains on the faculty there in Environmental and Occupational Health Sciences, as well as Mechanical Engineering. He serves on the Governing Board of the Illinois Council of Economic Education; on the Chicago Committee for the Chicago Council on Foreign Affairs; and on the Advisory Council for the Boy Scouts of America. He earned his undergraduate degree at Purdue University.

8

1930s

The walkway along the west side of the Quadrangle was known as

"the Boardwalk" during the University's early years

because wooden planks covered the dirt path.

With the widening and paving of the path later,

its name evolved to "the Broadwalk."

The Broadwalk has crowded with students from every era.

1929

Garland-B-

1930

1944

1948

1965

INTRODUCTION

The University of Illinois at Urbana-Champaign has a rich tradition of excellence in teaching, research and public service. As chancellor of this institution, I am confident that the flagship of the University of Illinois system also promises a future filled with accomplishment and advances that will help lead this nation into the coming century.

A brief glimpse into this campus' past, I hope, will serve to highlight the many ways in which the University of Illinois has affected the lives of millions of people around the globe. I hope that it also shows some of the personality and vision that make the Urbana-Champaign campus the heart of higher education in Illinois.

Since its opening in 1868, the University of Illinois at Urbana-Champaign has awarded more than 400,000 degrees. Our current enrollment of 35,000 dwarfs the original class of 77 students, who lived in a small dormitory above their classrooms and, on occasion, presented their assignments to professors while wearing their bed clothes. The muddy pastures that often forced students to cross campus in rubber boots eventually gave way to a beautiful, campus of buildings and facilities that span nearly 1,400 acres and provide space for students to work, study, live, and relax.

Michael Aiken

Over the years, the University of Illinois at Urbana-Champaign has fostered an environment that allows educators to teach, researchers to create, and dreamers to imagine the possibilities available through hard work and dedication. Those efforts have led to an array of firsts over the years: in 1872, we were the first institution in America to award an architecture degree; in 1914, we introduced the soybean as a potential crop for the Midwest; in 1940, a U of I researcher invented the betatron for high-energy physics; in 1959, our researchers developed PLATO, the first computer used for direct education; in 1981, a team here developed a new method for removing sulphur from Illinois coal. These examples are just a tiny fraction of the exciting innovations and ideas that have come to life on our campus. And those creations are but a portion of what makes the University of Illinois at Urbana-Champaign the state's premier public institution.

Although the University boasts so many impressive achievements that it would be impossible to illustrate each of them in this book, I hope you will see that our heritage also includes a personality that evolves with each graduating class. From the dancing cornstalks of the early 1900s May Fete to the 1980s hackey sack players on the Quad, our students find the right mix of scholarship, sportsmanship, community involvement, and fun. And they create formal and informal traditions that give the University a friendlier atmosphere than you might expect to find at a world-class research institution.

Many of our campus traditions have become so popular that other schools have imitated them, and they have become annual events all across the country. We are often credited with beginning such celebrations as Homecoming, Dad's Day, and Mom's Day, and with creating the institution of collegiate cheerleaders. Other traditions on campus may not be as long lasting, but for their duration, they are equally popular. Just ask anyone who ever tried to find a seat in Professor Paul Landis' classroom each year when he read Charles Dickens' *A Christmas Carol* to a packed room before the holiday break. Or talk with students a generation ago, who took great care not to step on the bronze plaque of the Gettysburg Address that adorned the floor of Lincoln Hall. Their side-stepping must have looked awkward to campus visitors, but students found nothing strange about the practice. Just as students eventually discarded that tradition, over the years they have created new ones to replace it, as well as others that faded out of style. That evolution illustrates the dynamic nature of the Urbana campus.

The international mix of our campus is another dimension that enhances the college experience for students as well as faculty and staff. In addition to our enrollees from 101 counties in Illinois, each of the 50 United States, the District of Columbia, and the territories of Guam and Puerto Rico, we also have students from 93 countries, from Albania to Zaire. This interchange allows each of our students the opportunity to learn about other cultures and traditions, preparing them to participate in the global workforce they will join after graduation.

The University of Illinois at Urbana-Champaign is a source of pride for people throughout this great state, but especially for residents of east central Illinois. In fact, without their efforts, it is unlikely that our campus would be located where it is. As lawmakers considered the best place to create this institution, they were strongly lobbied by leaders of Bloomington, Chicago, Jacksonville, Lincoln, and Normal. Competition was fierce at times, but Urbana's offer, including $50,000 in free freight on the Illinois Central Railroad and $2,000 in trees, shrubs, and other landscape materials, was enough to sway the decision-makers. We are certain they would still choose Urbana, and that they would be proud to see what has grown from their early vision.

The first regent of the University, John Milton Gregory, worked tirelessly to ensure that the University provided young people the opportunity to become productive members of society. Dr. Gregory is buried on campus, just south of Altgeld Hall. The marker at his gravesite reads, "If you seek his monument, look about you." After reading this book, I invite you to visit our campus and do that. You will find museums exhibiting treasures and history from all around the world; performing centers showcasing the talents of students, faculty, and others; athletic facilities featuring nationally ranked NCAA sports teams; and, of course, countless classrooms, laboratories, and libraries where learning and discovery happen each day. In short, you will find the state's premier educational center for those who will lead us into the coming century.

I hope that you enjoy your journey through our history, and I am delighted to invite you to share in our future.

Michael Aiken

Michael Aiken became Chancellor of the University of Illinois at Urbana-Champaign in July of 1993. Before becoming Chief Executive Officer of the UIUC campus, Dr. Aiken was Provost of the University of Pennsylvania—the chief academic officer of the Ivy League school, where he previously had served as Chair of the Sociology Department and Dean of the School of Arts and Sciences.

A widely published sociologist, Dr. Aiken has specialized in organizational behavior, with a focus on analysis of change in complex organizations. He has been active in professional organizations including the Midwest Sociological Society, American Sociological Association, International Sociological Association, and the Council for European Studies.

Apart from his nine years at Penn, Dr. Aiken's academic home has been in public universities: He is a graduate of the University of Mississippi, earned his doctorate from the University of Michigan, and served on the faculty of the University of Wisconsin at Madison for more than 21 years.

Foellinger Auditorium

Illini Union

Smith Memorial Hall

Detail, Smith Memorial Hall

Edward R. Madigan Laboratory

Main Library

Detail, Diana Fountain

Grainger Engineering Library Information Center

Harker Hall

Harker Hall

Undergraduate Library

Grainger Engineering Library
Information Center

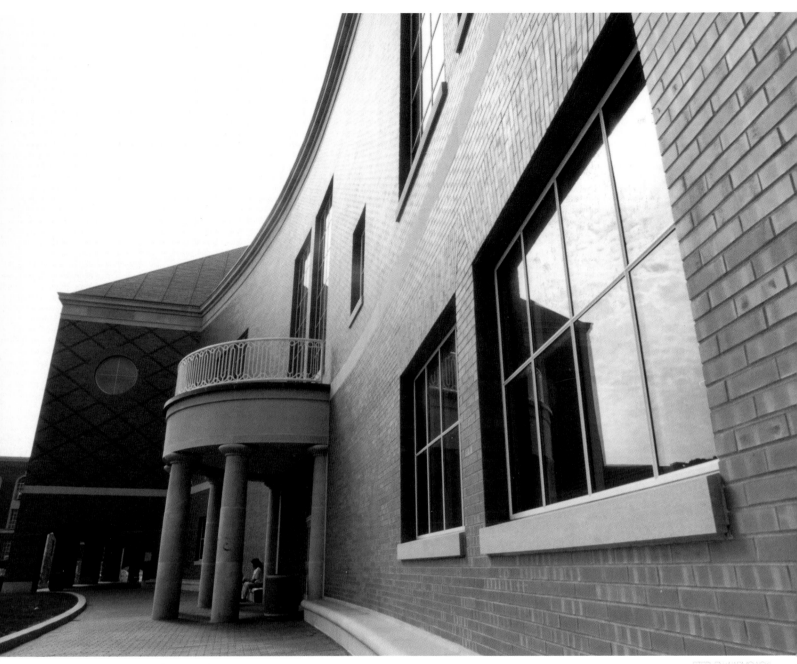

Grainger Engineering Library Information Center

Cupola; Illini Union

Altgeld Hall Tower

23

Wesley Foundation and
United Methodist Church

Hartley Gardens

Kinkead Pavilion, Krannert Art Museum

President's house

Interior, Beckman Institute for Advanced Science and Technology

Beckman Institute for Advanced Science and Technology

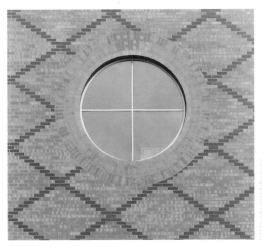

Detail, Grainger Engineering Library

Temple Hoyne Buell Hall

Chemical and Life Sciences Laboratory

Plant Sciences Laboratory

Robert Allerton House

Robert Allerton Park

English Building

Architecture

Stroll through campus in the
1870s, when livestock still roamed
the muddy prairie landscape.
Marvel at newly built Temple
Hoyne Buell Hall and the scientific
wonderland of the Beckman
Institute for Advanced Science
and Technology.

In 1952, I and my wife came from Tucumán, Argentina, to the University of Illinois with a scholarship from the Institute of National Education. It was our first time in the United States. It was an exciting and difficult period for us; we were fortunate to encounter some extraordinary people in Urbana-Champaign, within the student body and at the University. We made good friendships then that we still treasure.

There were two exceptional persons in the University to whom we owe our having been able to remain in the United States and have full professional lives here. One was Ambrose Richardson, head of the graduate program at the School of Architecture. He welcomed me—and us—not just as a student, but as a friend. He had left the firm of Skidmore Owings & Merrill a short time before my arrival, and from him I had my first understandings of the American system of architectural practice. Most importantly, he cared for me and my future. He provided me with my first opportunity in my architectural career in the United States by recommending me to the firm of Eero Saarinen and

Cesar Pelli

Associates, where I could apprentice with a good master and where my practice of architecture started.

The other person was Arthur Hamilton, dean of foreign students, a man of great intelligence and dedication who truly cared for his charges. My wife and I would have had to leave the United States if it were not for his willingness to battle the bureaucracy to solve our visa problems. He was the kind of person who transforms routine administrative positions into a vocation, a creative act of service to those who desperately need it. When he retired it was as if night had come for the foreign students. A few persons like Arthur Hamilton in critical positions can give life to an institution.

We spent two years at the University of Illinois, and to us, Urbana-Champaign was the United States. Although we were living in the most penurious circumstances, with a newborn son and continuous tribulations, I remember those years at the University of Illinois as some of the richest and happiest years of my life.

Cesar Pelli M.*Arch* '54

A Fellow of the American Institute of Architects, Cesar Pelli M.Arch '54, is a noted practitioner, author, and scholar in his field. He earned the 1995 Gold Medal of the American Institute of Architects, the profession's highest honor, for a lifetime of distinguished achievement and outstanding contributions. His award-winning designs include the World Financial Center and Winter Garden in New York; the Pacific Design Center in Los Angeles; and the United States Embassy in Tokyo, Japan. Mr. Pelli founded Cesar Pelli & Associates in 1977, and the firm was recognized by the American Institute of Architects in 1989 for contributing over a decade of standard-setting work in architectural design.

Illini Hall, built in 1908 as the YMCA, was the first
home of the Illinois Union organization.

The Sunken
Rock Garden,
near the
Observatory,
flourished from
1916 to 1961.

Willard
Airport, 1945.

Student Army
Training Corps
in front of the
Armory, built
in 1914.

The Computer and Systems Research Laboratory, North Quad, completed in 1992.

The Krannert Center for the Performing Arts and Krannert Art Museum were gifts of Herman Krannert '12, and his wife, Ellnora. Architect Max Abramovitz '29, shaped the concert hall and three theaters of the Krannert Center to provide first-rate acoustics and facilities for music, drama, opera and dance performances. The center opened in 1969.

White Vermont marble, gold-plated window screens and an abstract bronze sculpture, *Initiation*, distinguished the Krannert Art Museum, dedicated in 1961. In the early 1990s, the reflecting pool was replaced with gardens.

The only Romanesque building on campus, Altgeld Hall was constructed of rough-hewn pink sandstone in 1897 to house the University Library. Architect Nathan Ricker completed his studies at the University in 1872 to become the first architecture graduate in the country. The tower's chimes, dedicated in 1920, have beckoned to generations of students. Inside the rotunda, columns and intricately patterned paintings and murals enrich the flavor of the building.

The Illini Union became the front door of the campus in 1941, built on the site of University Hall. Its Georgian architecture was inspired by colonial Williamsburg, Virginia. The 30-foot cupola on the front section of the building houses the University's historic chapel bell and a clock from University Hall, a gift of the class of 1878. The south wing of the Union was added in 1961.

Buell Hall became the new home of the architecture, urban
planning, and landscape architecture programs in 1995. Its
benefactor was Temple Hoyne Buell '16, a well-known architect.

The Observatory was constructed in 1896 on land that had
been part of the Morrow Plots. The building is now a National
Historic Landmark.

The twin towers, stately columns, and dormer windows of the English Building mark a classic period of University architecture just after the turn of the century. It was originally called the Woman's Building and was used as a gym and meeting place.

The Morrow Plots, a continuous experiment since 1876.

The pillar and bench located near the English Building were given as a memorial by the class of 1912. Campus legend predicts that couples who kiss on the bench are destined for marriage.

The Beckman Institute for Advanced Science and Technology, dedicated in 1989, was a gift of Dr. Arnold O. Beckman '22, MS '23, and his wife, Mabel. The red brick and green glass wonderland unites biological and physical scientists in a quest for understanding of human and artificial intelligence.

Smith Memorial Hall, completed in 1920, was the first University building constructed without state funds. Thomas J. Smith, an attorney and University trustee, financed the building as a memorial to his wife, Tina. It follows the campus' classical style with a temple-like facade.

Italianate-style Harker Hall opened in 1878 as one of the premier chemistry laboratories in the nation. University architect Nathan Ricker *1872, M.Arch. 1878*, used Kankakee and Joliet limestone topped by a black slate mansard roof. Ravaged by time and fires, the oldest classroom building on campus was restored to its original grandeur in 1992 and now serves as headquarters of the University of Illinois Foundation.

Lorado Taft *1879, ML 1880*, originally envisioned his bronze statue *Alma Mater* being placed on the front steps of the Auditorium, and a plaster cast perched there for a time during 1922.

The first University President's house, built in the early 1900s, was situated at Wright and Green streets.

The Lily Pond was established on South Campus in 1916 and filled in 1961.

The six-year-old campus of the "Illinois Industrial University" looked much like the pasture that preceded it. Looking north from University Hall, students in 1874 saw Green Street, Boneyard Creek, the Drill Hall, and, dominating the horizon, the University's old Main Building, which they dubbed "the Elephant." The two top floors of the Elephant, seen below, served as dormitories, while the rest of the building housed classrooms, a chapel, and student club rooms. Students spent their mandatory two hours of daily manual labor beautifying its grounds.

Completed in 1926, McKinley Health Center is named for Senator William
B. McKinley, whose gift financed its construction.

Philanthropist and art collector Robert Allerton gave his stately 40-room English Georgian mansion and more than 5,000 acres of surrounding gardens, woodlands, and cropland near Monticello to the University in 1946.

Originally located on Green Street in front of University Hall, the Halfway House may have been so named because it stood halfway between the business districts of Urbana and Champaign. The century-old structure previously served as a waiting stop for the Urbana & Champaign Electric Street Railway and is now a bus shelter on Matthews Street.

Aerial view of the main Quad, 1984.

Flying saucer-shaped Assembly Hall, 1963, was designed by Max Abramovitz '29.

Memorial Stadium, 1924, honors the nearly 200 Illini who died in World War I. It was built with $2 million in donations from students, faculty, alumni, and friends of the University.

Plans for the Main Library, built in 1926, included room to house an ever-growing collection in future expansions. Additions have formed the "Stacks" at the rear of the building. The Undergraduate Library, foreground, was built underground in 1968 so as not to block sunlight on the Morrow Plots. It is connected to the Main Library via a tunnel.

As the first regent of the Illinois Industrial University, John Milton Gregory laid the foundations for the University's success. His undying dedication is evident in his wish to remain on campus forever, in a grave near Altgeld Hall. The 3,300-pound stone that marks his grave instructs those who come after him: "If you seek his monument, look about you."

Round barns were built on the South Farms in 1912 and 1913 to house dairy cattle.

Victorian-style
University Hall
was built in 1874
and demolished
in 1938. It stood
on the site of the
present Illini Union.

Illinois Street
Residence Halls,
erected in 1964.

Converted army
barracks from
Indiana, the Parade
Ground Units and
Stadium Terrace
housing complexes
were quickly
assembled near
Memorial Stadium
after World War II
to accommodate
veteran students and
their families.

The Forestry, near present-day Pennsylvania and Lincoln avenues, started in 1871 as a forest research project. This 1910 photo shows the extent of the stand of trees, the remnants of which now exist in Illini Grove.

University President Andrew Draper tried to polish the image of Boneyard Creek by renaming it Silver Creek around the turn of the century.

The Natural History Building, completed in 1893.

Completed in 1912, Lincoln Hall is a tribute to the central Illinois lawyer who went on to lead the nation and sign the Land-Grant Act that was the start of the University. The building's white terra-cotta frieze depicts Abraham Lincoln's life.

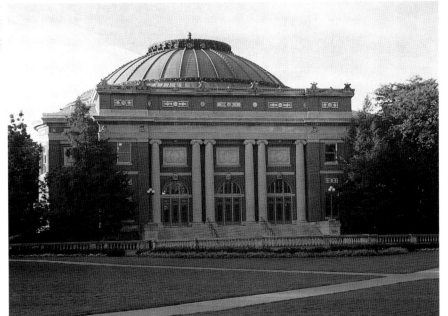

Though construction on the Auditorium stopped in 1908, the complete plans of architect Clarence Blackall *1877, M.Arch. 1880*, were not fulfilled until the building was restored in 1985. It was then renamed Foellinger Auditorium for the benefactress of the restoration, alumna Helene Foellinger *'32*, a newspaper publisher and communications industry executive.

Academics

Study in University Hall in the 1890s, in the Main Library in the 1950s, and in Grainger Engineering Library Information Center in the 1990s. Meet professors who have pioneered the frontiers of human knowledge and scholarship in agriculture, computing, physics, engineering, and other fields.

Since 1940, the University of Illinois has been the focus of my professional life. I enrolled that fall as a first-year law student in Altgeld Hall with a newly minted bachelor of arts degree from Illinois Wesleyan University. A great faculty of law quickly convinced me that I was in the right place and the right discipline. The distant war drums in Europe were sounding a different beat, however, and in May of 1941 I began a four and one-half-year stint in the U.S. Army with a year and a half (1943-45) in the European theater of operations. The academic life and the legal profession seemed part of another, and alien, world. The atomic age wrote finis to World War II and hurried me back to Altgeld Hall, where the dean at that time, Albert Harno, came to attention and saluted each returning veteran as he visited individually with us in his office and chatted about the missing years on campus. The entire law faculty participated in review sessions and updated us on the, by then, stale learning of four or five years before. Illinois may have been a huge, impersonal university to some, but the warmth of those post-war years showed our generation that there was a deep faculty concern for our welfare and our careers. I knew then that I would be proud to be a part of such an institution.

John Cribbet

It was my good fortune that Dean Harno and the faculty asked me, in 1947, to join with them in the great adventure that is higher education. So, after a brief period in private practice, I became a colleague of my former professors and embarked on an academic legal career. Although I centered in the College of Law, I quickly found my activities to be campus wide. I served on committees and in the Faculty Senate and began to see the University as a whole and to realize that, in fact, the University of Illinois was one of the world's leading centers of higher education.

Although teaching, research, and writing were my primary interests, I gradually discovered that administration, too, had its appeal, and this led to twelve years as dean of the College of Law and five years as chancellor of the Urbana-Champaign campus. They were fascinating years of growth and change, of student unrest, troops on the campus, athletic problems (remember the Wilson case?), and so forth. Except for the years of "chancelling," I continued to teach, and even in those years I tried to teach in a different way, without formal classes but with maximum student contact. As chancellor, I felt I had a firm grip on the tiller, but no conviction that it was connected to the rudder. Perhaps that is as it should be since this great Land-Grant institution has a momentum all of its own and will continue to forge ahead, under ever-renewing leadership, on into the new century. The past *is* forever prologue, and with such a distinguished past, the future for the University of Illinois is bright indeed.

John Cribbet *JD '47*

John E. Cribbet JD '47, joined the College of Law in 1947 as Assistant Professor. Since then, he has served the University in numerous administrative, organizational, and co-curricular capacities. From 1967 through 1979, he was Dean of the College of Law and for five years after that served as Chancellor of the Urbana - Champaign campus. In addition to the titles of Dean and Chancellor Emeritus, Mr. Cribbet also holds the rank of Corman Professor of Law Emeritus and continues to teach in the college.

The Main Library Reference Room was a popular place to study in 1953.

The University is a leader in providing learning resources for disabled students.

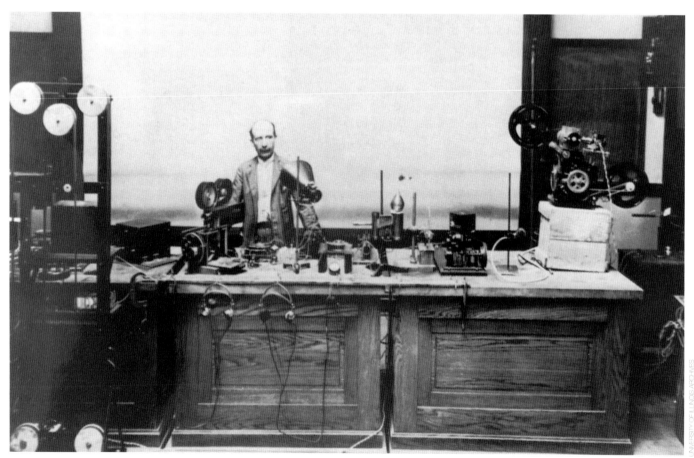

Engineering Professor Joseph Tykociner invented the recording of sound on film. The first "talking movie" debuted at a University laboratory on June 9, 1922.

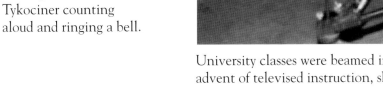

Film strip of the world's first sound movie, starring Helena Tykociner counting aloud and ringing a bell.

University classes were beamed into homes with the advent of televised instruction, shown here in 1959.

The Arboretum provided an ideal setting for students to practice surveying in 1890.

Computerization of the registration process in 1995 ended last-minute scheduling in the Armory at the start of every semester, as shown here in the 1970s.

The Morrow Plots were instrumental in proving that prairie soil can be depleted by continuous corn cropping and that crop rotation helps prevent soil exhaustion. These men compared ears in 1960.

University researchers devoted more than four decades to introducing soybeans as a major crop in the United States. Soybeans were first planted in the University greenhouse in 1903 and now are second only to corn in value to the U.S. agricultural economy.

Entomology laboratory, University Hall, 1889.

Classics Professor Richard Scanlan breathes life into his lectures by portraying mythological characters, complete with appropriate costumes.

In 1925, the University conducted a corn judging course in nearby Monticello, Illinois.

The 1953 Engineering Open House included a "Kiss-O-Meter," along with demonstration offers.

Test taking, 1963.

In 1946, this large English class was populated primarily by women.

Physiology students posed their laboratory skeleton for this photo in 1902.

A virtual reality laboratory at the University's National Center for Supercomputing Applications (NCSA) helped this graduate student view molecular dynamics in 1992.

The University's world-famous National Center for Supercomputing Applications focuses on creating advanced computing and communication tools and information technologies, including the data visualization software above.

Studying, 1970s.

Engineering Professor Arthur C. Willard, later University President, solved one of the great engineering problems of the early twentieth century by developing the principles for a ventilation system for the Holland Tunnel between New York City and New Jersey.

Studying, 1915.

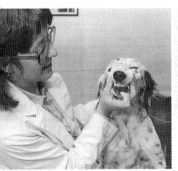

Veterinary medicine student and patient, 1963.

At the 1960 U of I Farm and Home Festival, a Geiger counter traced the path of radioactive nutrients through a goat.

In 1940, Professor Donald W. Kerst built the world's first betatron, a machine that produces cosmic ray energies. The betatron creates x-rays used to treat cancers and z-rays for pinpointing flaws in complicated industrial machinery through photography, and has also prompted many discoveries concerning atoms.

First of the University's famous scientists, Thomas J. Burrill taught the nation's first class in microscopic organisms, discovered that bacteria cause plant disease, and served as University regent for three years. With him in the Bacteriological Lab in 1888 were Freda Detmer, middle, and Annetta Ayers Saunders 1884, right.

Researchers prepare to measure the results of dropping a concrete pillar in the four-story testing machine at the Materials Testing Laboratory in 1937.

Students have gazed at the skies from the Observatory since 1896, making it one of the nation's oldest observatories still in use.

Distillation experiment, Noyes Lab, 1958.

Late-night studying in 1967 included coffee, cigarettes and hair curlers.

68

Home economics students timed a pressure cooker while canning in a foods laboratory in the 1940s.

The names of the graduating seniors with the highest grade
averages are enshrined each year on bronze tablets that line
the hallways of the Main Library.

Studying microscopic organisms, 1948.

Checking job interview schedules at the Illini Union, 1970.

Instructor Frances B. Jenkins taught the periodic table to students in 1951.

Margaret O'Donnell '48 became the first female graduate of the Department of Mining and Metallurgical Engineering. Department head H.L. Walker joined her here.

Home Economics Professor Isabel Bevier headed the federal Home Economics Advisory Committee when President Herbert Hoover took over the nation's food economy during World War I.

Organic chemist Roger Adams served the government as a researcher during both world wars. Among his students at Illinois was Wallace Carothers MS '21, PHD '24, nylon inventor.

Microbiology Professor Carl Woese discovered a third form of life, archaebacteria, in 1977.

Professor Fred Gottheil brought economics to life in this 1987 lecture.

71

Professor Stephen A. Forbes developed the concept of "ecosystem" in 1887, laying the foundations for applied ecology and pest management.

Professor John Bardeen twice shared the Nobel Prize in physics, for inventing the transistor and for developing the theory of superconductivity.

In 1959, Engineering Professor Don Bitzer began developing PLATO, the first computer used for direct education. After serving serious students during the day, the PLATO laboratories attract dozens of game players every night.

These women went through the ritual of buying books in 1964.

Chemistry Professor William Rose, left, discovered the amino acids essential for human nutrition in the 1940s. He received the Willard Gibbs Medal of the American Chemical Society for his work.

In 1955, students worked with cumbersome digital computers.

Studying, 1890.

Law Professor Edward Cleary drafted the Rules of Evidence, enacted by Congress in 1975 and since applied by all courts in the United States.

Plaster casts served as models for students practicing drawing in the Architecture Building's Hall of Casts in the 1930s.

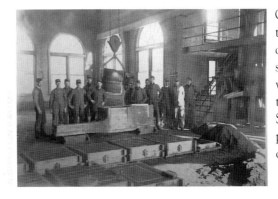

Opened in 1869, the Foundry was one of the first such student workshops in the nation. Student work paid the Foundry's operating costs.

Sewing was a part of the "household science" curriculum in 1930.

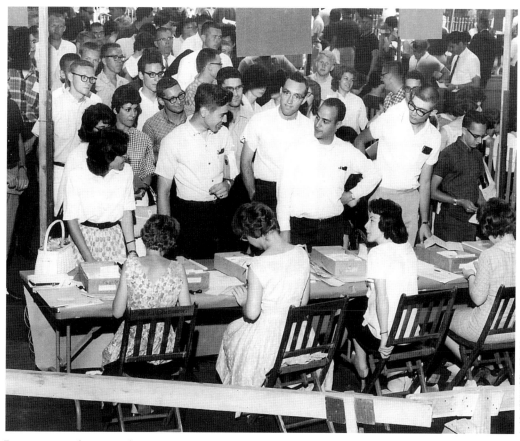

Registration lines in the Armory, 1963.

Future farmers learned about Hampshire hogs in 1958.

Sheep judging classes were offered at the Stock Pavilion after the turn of the century.

Illini Nellie, the world champion Brown Swiss milk
producer, drew a crowd of state legislators in the 1920s.

Principal's Scholars Program, 1986.

Stanley Ikenberry
served as University
President for 16 years
stepping down in 1995.

Student Life

Cheer at pushball contests, reminisce at soda fountains, and bunk in the dormitories with students from the past century. Witness how the campus and its students responded to the wars that have shaped the nation during the twentieth century.

On Saturday mornings, I love to throw on my favorite orange and blue sweatshirt and a warm pair of mittens, grabbing a mug of hot chocolate as I take off out the door. As several friends and I set out across campus, we know we are nearing the right place when we start to smell hamburgers, see streams of traffic, and hear the Marching Illini coming down the street. Another Big Ten game is about to begin, and fans are already cheering, "I-L-L, I-N-I!" Witnessing tailgaters of all ages, including alumni, students, and children, who have come to root for the team gives me a content feeling all over. The pride and loyalty felt toward the University of Illinois are never more evident than on game days, and it is those days that compose my fondest memories of Illinois.

I started visiting the University in my early teens because I had friends here who were students. I can remember the first time they took me to the Quad and how awed I was by the sight. If I stood right in the middle, I had Foellinger Auditorium to one side of me and the Union to the other, with many gorgeous buildings in between. The campus seemed overwhelming at the time, but after coming to Illinois for my own education I learned that it wasn't so monstrous after all. Now, a quick four years later, I even feel as if the campus has shrunk, and I no longer have to guess which building is which.

Jennifer Sherlock

In fact, the University really is a very small world. With over 700 registered organizations, it's easy to find students who share your interests, whether reading poetry, bicycling or re-enacting knightly battles. In addition, the Urbana-Champaign community is integrated with the campus environment, providing opportunities ranging from after-school tutoring to volunteering in the hospital emergency room.

No matter what the interest, the U of I seems to come through, at least it always has for me. I know that I am getting one of the best educations possible. I have had excellent opportunities to improve upon my leadership abilities through participation in a wide range of activities; I have been impressed with the fact that we have the largest Greek system and celebrate the nation's oldest Homecoming; and most importantly, I know that whether a student or an alumna, I can still grab that warm drink, throw on my Illini apparel, and go cheer for the team! Entering the University was the best decision I have made. I will always be happy knowing that I am a part of something that has been around long before I came and will remain in the highest standing long after I am gone.

Jennifer Sherlock '96

Jennifer Sherlock '96, is a senior from Godfrey, Illinois, who is majoring in chemistry and applying to medical school. On campus, she is involved in the Student Alumni Association as president, Mortar Board, her social sorority, and Sachem Junior Honorary. She also teaches science to elementary-age children and volunteers at Carle Hospital in Urbana.

This couple sat on the rail in front of Foellinger Auditorium in 1989.

80

Students in their dormitory room in the 1940s.

The Rifle and Pistol Club of
1930-31 was exclusively
female except for the advisers.

Fraternity houses became Army barracks during World War II. These soldiers bunked in the Sigma Pi fraternity living room.

The Armory was called "the biggest bedroom in the state" during World War I, housing 2,000 student soldiers and a mess hall.

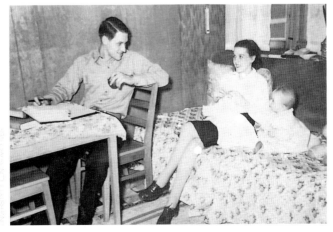

After World War II, the University accommodated an influx of married students and their children.

Women marched on campus for the first time in 1943, as members of the Army's Women's Auxiliary Training Corps.

Hired bicycles were popular on dates during the 1920s.

Military training was required of all male students until 1891, when upperclassmen were excused. Wearing cadet-gray uniforms, this company practiced by the Drill Hall in 1889.

Military Day observance on the Quad during World War I.

Hundreds of students gathered on the Quad in the spring of 1978 to welcome the arrival of four parachuting streakers.

The Student Alumni Association fed a hungry mob during "Lunch on the Quad" celebrating Homecoming Week 1994.

Pushball was a popular inter-class competition in the 1910s, until it was canceled due to the danger of injury. The sophomores beat the freshmen in this 1912 match.

Library science students competed in softball in 1969.

This student dressed down to celebrate Homecoming 1925 in the once-traditional Hobo Parade.

Throughout the 1980s, preacher Max Lynch spent many days on the Quad trying to "save the souls" of students.

Tricycle races on the Quad, 1994.

Playing pool at the Illini Union, 1970.

Beard-growing contest, 1930.

A welcome sight on a snowy day in 1962, Illi-Buses served University students, faculty and staff.

The patio of the Illini Union has served as a forum for opinions, protests, and performances since it was built in 1967 for the centennial of the University's charter.

Rinsing off after a mud volleyball game, 1987.

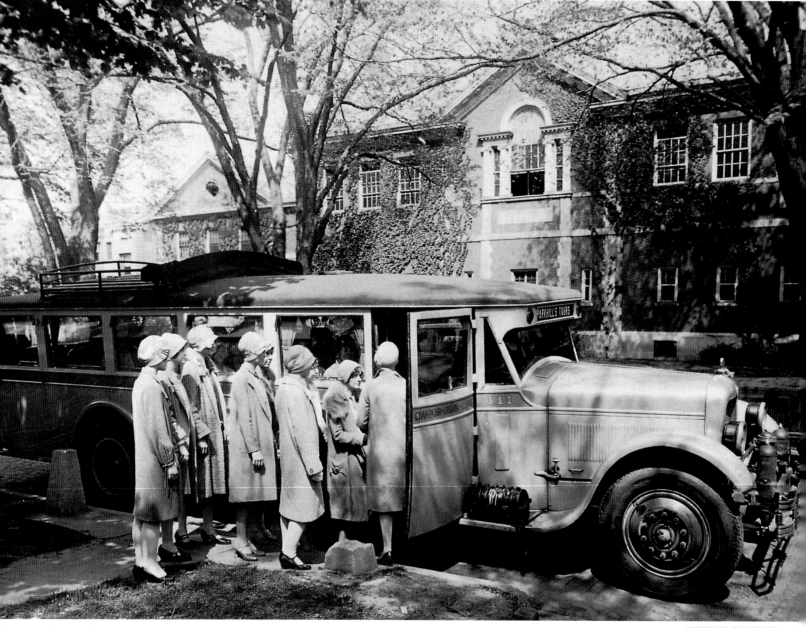

Fashionable coeds boarding a bus, circa 1924.

Moving into the
dormitories, 1977.

A soon-to-be graduate packed
her belongings in 1945.

Courtship, 1940s.

Greek Week, 1961.

Aviator Amelia Earhart, right, was hosted on campus in 1935
by Sarah Willard, wife of University President Arthur C. Willard.

President William Taft reviewed troops
of student cadets at Illinois Field in 1911.

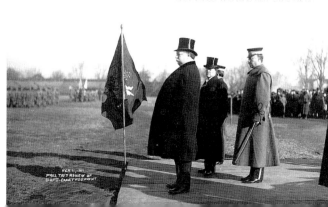

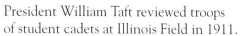

Presidential candidate John F. Kennedy campaigned on Wright Street in 1960.

Hackey sacks became popular entertainment for students on the Quad beginning in the 1980s.

The 1978 "Fiji Party" at Phi Gamma Delta fraternity inspired island attire.

Puppeteer Stephen Baird and his friend, Pierre, entertained students on the Quad annually during the 1980s and '90s.

Fraternity men serenading a sorority, 1955.

In 1967, the Red Herring Coffeehouse opened in the Channing-Murray Foundation building on Oregon Street. The popular hangout was known for its spring and fall folk festivals and for launching the career of singer Dan Fogelberg.

Offers of all kinds could be found on campus bulletin boards, 1970s.

The Chase Club on Wright Street housed male and female students for more than a decade, including these 1892 boarders. Boarding clubs were centers for lodging, dining, and socializing, especially before the construction of the first University residence halls—for women in 1908 and for men in 1942.

Prehn's opened on the corner of Oregon Street and Goodwin Avenue in the late 1920s. With the decor of a Spanish villa, it was one of the most popular hang-outs on campus.

Hanging out at the Willard Airport snack bar, circa 1950.

This mural appears in La Casa Cultural Latina, a center for Latin art, culture, friendships and activities.

Pinball machines in the Illini Union were heavily used during 1975.

The Daily Illini newspaper
has been the voice of
students for 125 years.

Hurrying to get ready for
class, 1987.

Awaiting a train
home for the
holidays, 1981.

Seesawing, 1910.

Canoes on Crystal Lake in Urbana, 1939.

Walking to classes in the rain, 1985.

Without laundromats, students in the 1880s either mailed their laundry home or had it picked up by a laundry service such as that of "Red" Donohew, making a stop here at the Natural History Building.

The Cosmopolitan Club attracted students from several countries in the 1910s.

In the fall of 1969, 9,000 opponents of the Vietnam War marched to Westside Park in Champaign in a demand for peace. The following spring, the National Guard was called to campus during a week of unruly protests.

Protesters marched down Green Street in 1969.

In 1968, student protesters wore black armbands signifying
people killed in the still-raging Vietnam War.

Arts & Entertainment

Attend world-class professional and student productions in the Lincoln Hall Auditorium, Foellinger Auditorium, Illini Union, and Krannert Center for the Performing Arts. Visit campus museums that house dinosaur skeletons, mummies, and famous works of art.

Growing up in Chicago in the 1920s and '30s provided me with many opportunities, especially in the area of the arts. My parents, both immigrants from Italy, brought their brand of a cultural environment with them and established it in our home. We were treated to operas, museums and art galleries, concerts by the Works Progress Administration Symphony Orchestra, and unforgettable vaudeville productions accompanying first-rate movies in beautiful art deco theaters.

My musical career started with the encouragement of my parents and lessons at Hull House, which is now a National Historic Landmark on the University's Chicago campus. I played at weddings and parties, earning wages for my efforts. Later my performances expanded to Chicago ballrooms and nightclubs, then elsewhere with regional bands and orchestras.

Driving to the University in Urbana in the fall of 1940, I began to wonder what my life would be like away from the wonders of Chicago, which offered its citizens a banquet of cultural resources. I was aware of the magnificence of the University's Concert Band, for it was my reason for wanting to matriculate at the U of I.

Daniel Perrino

I soon learned that even though the campus was comparatively small by today's standards (12,500 students in 1940 grew to approximately 35,000 in 1995), it was not a cultural desert.

The University boasted the premier band program in the nation. Under the direction of A.A. Harding '06, the bands provided the campus community ample opportunities to hear the music of the masters, including John Philip Sousa. School of Music students performed in the Recital Hall of Smith Memorial Hall and in the Auditorium. Star Course, our student-run concert and entertainment organization, brought world-famous artists to rural Illinois—performers such as Dame Myra Hess, Charles Laughton, Helen Hayes, Enzio Pinza, and more.

After World War II, the University faced a ballooning population of students, many of them married veterans with new-found global tastes in culture. The University responded to the arts and entertainment needs of students with the Krannert Art Museum, Assembly Hall, and, the most ambitious project on campus, the Krannert Center for the Performing Arts, dedicated in 1969. The Krannert Center remains one of the outstanding centers for the performing arts on any campus in the world, and practically every major performer has appeared on one of its four stages. Rounding out cultural offerings during my musical tenure were the Japan House's presentation of Asian culture and Kabuki theatre, the Kinkead Pavilion addition to the art museum, and the World Heritage Museum with its ancient art objects.

My fears back in 1940 of coming to a cultural wasteland were certainly unfounded. The University has played and continues to play a leadership role in presenting a wide variety of arts and entertainment to the thousands of students, faculty, and staff who pass through the campus. From Presley to Pavarotti, from circuses to ballet; from cartoons to oil paintings; from comedy to Shakespeare; and from jazz to classics—it's been here and continues just for the asking.

Marching Band King John Philip Sousa, at left on opposite page, was a friend of University Concert Band Director A.A. Harding, '06 right. Sousa visited campus several times and once directed the Marching Band. His handwritten scores and music stand are preserved in the Harding Band Building.

Daniel Perrino '48, MS '49

Daniel J. Perrino '48, MS '49, Professor of Music Emeritus, has been a part of the University as a member of the faculty and administrative staff for approximately forty years. He has served as Director of Music Extension in the School of Music; Dean of Student Programs and Services; and Associate Dean of the College of Fine and Applied Arts. He is a founding member of the Dixieland jazz band Medicare 7, 8, or 9. Mr. Perrino now serves as Assistant to the Director of the University of Illinois Alumni Association.

One of the first educational television stations, WILL-TV went on the air in 1955 from makeshift studios under the Memorial Stadium stands. Meanwhile, the forerunner of the Public Broadcasting System was germinating in the basement of Gregory Hall.

In 1967, the University Theatre troupe staged its productions in the Lincoln Hall Auditorium.

Star Course, a student-run production and promotion company since 1891, brought Louis Armstrong to campus in the 1950s.

The now-forgotten ritual of crowning the May Queen was started
by the Women's League in 1899. Here, the 1910 queen reigns.

The sixth annual Twilight Concert on the Quad was
in 1916, when cars were still allowed on the dirt path
bordering the lawn.

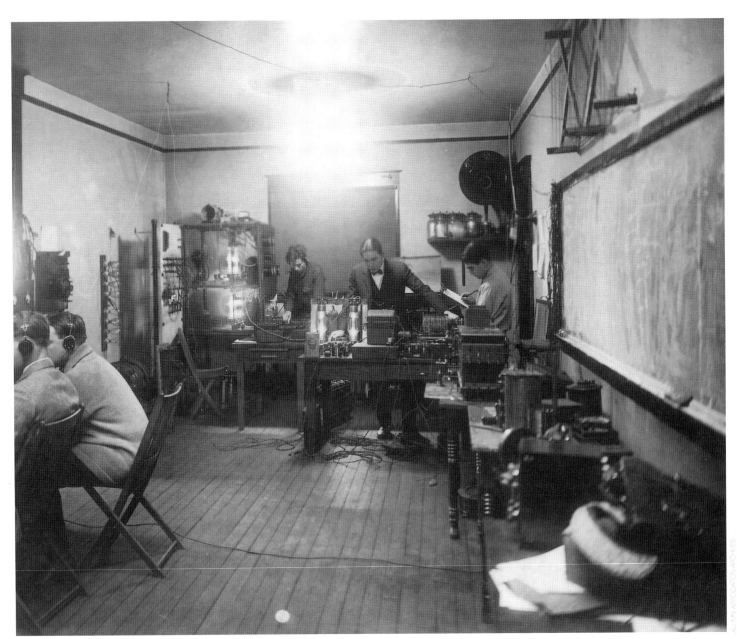

WILL, originally named WRM, began regular
radio broadcasts in 1922.

Krannert Art Museum, 1988.

The Illinois Dance
Theatre performed
Sanctuary by
Bebe Miller in 1993.

Women's Glee Club, 1967.

Gymkana, a traveling performance troupe, developed from the Interscholastic Circus. In 1940, members included roller skaters and gymnasts.

Guitar, Glee, and Mandolin clubs were wildly popular prior to the turn of the century, despite professors' insistence that music had no place in collegiate studies.

The Registration Dance was an icebreaker at the start of the 1965 academic year.

These students modeled traditional Chinese
wedding attire at the 1980 International Fair
in the Illini Union.

The "man with the golden flute," James Galway performed at the Krannert Center for Performing Arts in the 1990s.

An instructor for the Illini Martial Arts Club impressed the crowd at Quad Day 1985.

117

The Insect Fear Film Festival has combined insect-theme movies with live critters since the 1980s.

A graduate student wiped the brow of the
god Hermes at the World Heritage Museum
in Lincoln Hall in 1982.

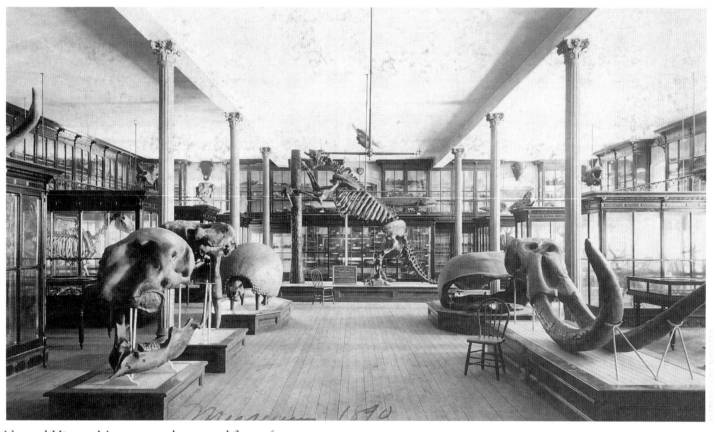

Natural History Museum on the second floor of
University Hall, 1890.

The Celestial Hemisphere is
one of four Art Deco murals by
Barry Faulkner hanging in the
Main Library staircases.

An Egyptian diorama at the World
Heritage Museum in Lincoln Hall
depicts the birth of writing.

The Concert Band started in 1890 with seven
players. It quickly grew in size and popularity,
performing annually in the Auditorium after the
turn of the century.

Conductor Bernard Goodman rehearsed the University
Symphony Orchestra in 1969.

The Illinois Opera Theatre performed
Mozart's *The Marriage of Figaro*
in 1993.

The Tony Zamora Ensemble gave concerts in the residence halls in 1969.

Star Course hosted Sly and the Family Stone at Assembly Hall in the 1970s.

W. B. Petty looked deceptively ladylike in the 1930 Pierrot production of *Brazil Nuts*. The exclusively male Pierrot organization thrived on campus from 1910 through the Great Depression, performing original student musicals in lavish feminine costumes.

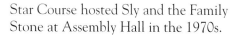

Orchesis, a student modern dance group
showed off its talents in 1956.

Dancing ears of corn, milkmaids, witches,
and fairies enlivened the 1915 May Fete.

The Men's Glee Club sang at the Krannert Center for the Performing Arts, 1988.

The International Banquet started at the University YMCA and later expanded in the Illini Union. This 1948 banquet at the Y's Latzer Hall focused on Latin American cultures.

The name of Dixieland jazz band Medicare 7, 8, or 9 was inspired by the advancing ages of its players and by the fluctuating number of them who appear at performances. The band, mostly University-affiliated musicians, has played throughout the country since its start in 1969.

A wooden sculpture called *The Family* by
John L. Vogt MFA '63, brought culture into
Garner Hall in 1964.

Composer Harry Partch
brought his unique
instruments to campus for
the premiere of his dance
satire *The Bewitched* at the
University's 1957 Festival of
Contemporary Arts. His
"cloud-chamber bowls"
had been previously used
in nuclear experiments.

Eleanor Roosevelt, widow of President Franklin D.
Roosevelt, was interviewed on WILL Radio in 1956.

127

*How to Succeed in Business Without Really
Trying,* a 1987 Illini Union show.

A VERNON

Athletics

Travel back to the days when basketball was a women's sport, when Illinois was the first university to celebrate Homecoming, and when the first Chief Illiniwek danced at a football game. Cheer the triumphs of the latest generation of Illini, including Olympian Sharon Rahn Hedrick, professional basketball player Kendall Gill, and baseball All-Star Darrin Fletcher.

When I arrived on campus in the fall of 1956, I saw an item in *The Daily Illini* that the basketball team was looking for managers. I walked over to Huff Gym, where the Fighting Illini played in those days, and signed up. That began a four-year involvement with Coach Harry Combes that had a tremendous impact on me. I developed lasting friendships with people like Mannie Jackson and Jerry Colangelo. I still remember the train trips to Evanston for the Northwestern games and the bus trips to Purdue when Coach Combes and I were bridge partners against all comers.

The influence of the University extended to my entire life. I met my wife, Kathy, during a Sigma Chi–Chi Omega exchange. Our oldest child, Susan, was born in Urbana while I was in grad school. I received my commission in the United States Marine Corps through the national Reserve Officers Training Corps program at Illinois. Both of my degrees are from the University of Illinois.

I think it is fair to say that I would never have attained the level of success I have enjoyed in the television industry without the foundation that I received while attending school in Urbana-Champaign. I will always be grateful to my alma mater.

Dennis Swanson

I once heard someone criticize the University of Illinois for being too large. But I learned to compete in that environment, which was essential preparation for what was to come later in the business world.

Big? Yes. Impersonal? No. I still recall coming back to school after my Marine Corps service to resume work toward a master's degree. Kathy was eight months pregnant when we moved into Orchard Downs on a scorching hot Sunday in June 1963. When I opened the refrigerator, it was filled with food from my college adviser. The accompanying note read, "Welcome Home Big Den."

Dennis Swanson '61, MS '66

In 1892 a hurdles runner drew a crowd at the University's first athletics stands.

Dennis Swanson '61, MS '66, is President of ABC Sports. He started in sports and broadcasting as a University student, working part-time at WILL television and radio stations. He was appointed to his present position in 1986 and, from 1991 through 1993, also served as President of ABC Daytime and ABC Children's Programming.

Basketball Team Manager Dennis Swanson was pictured in the "Campus Leaders" section of the 1960 *Illio*.

130

In the early 1900s, basketball was considered a sport exclusively for women.

The 1910 football team had a perfect season; it was never beaten and never scored upon.

On October 30, 1926, Lester Leutwiler '29, was the first student to dance as the University's Chief Illiniwek.

U·OF·I 1910.   1000% TEAM

The first university Homecoming in the nation was held at Illinois Field on October 15, 1910. The Illini beat Chicago 3-0.

George Halas '18, founded the Decatur Staleys, the football team that would later become the Chicago Bears.

1952 Homecoming Queen
Patti Ryden '55, reacts to
a congratulatory kiss.

Nancy Thies Marshall '79, earned fame
as the youngest American gymnast
competing in the 1972 Olympics, when
she was 14. In 1978, she wore the crown
of the Illinois Homecoming Queen.

Korean student
Duck Choo Oh
'56, center, was
crowned
Homecoming
Queen in 1955.

The Fighting Illini of 1891 included the University's second-ever football team and athletes from a variety of other sports.

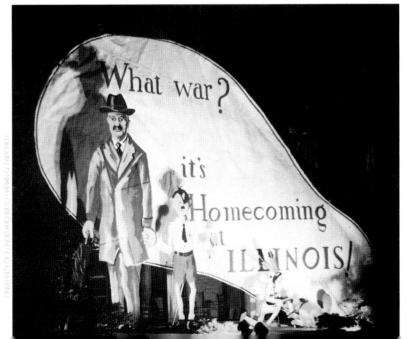

Beginning in the 1910s campus houses were elaborately decorated for Homecoming festivities.

Tennis team, 1912.

The Illini upset UCLA 45-14 to bring home the University's first Rose Bowl championship in 1947.

Fencing, 1964.

Football Coach Ray Eliot BS '32, himself a letter winner in football and baseball, brought home three Big Ten championships and two Rose Bowl titles.

The Illinois Sports Hall of Fame includes, from left, George Halas '18, founder and coach of the Chicago Bears; Doug Mills '30, coach of the 1943 Whiz Kids basketball team; Dwight "Dike" Eddleman '49, three-sport letter winner and Olympic high jumper; Harold "Red" Grange '26, Illini and professional football star; Bobby Richards '47, Olympic pole vaulter; Lou Boudreau '40, Illini and professional baseball star; and Kenneth "Tug" Wilson '20, Big Ten commissioner from 1945 to 1961.

137

Basketball star Kendall Gill '90, launched his professional career with the Charlotte Hornets.

John "Red" Kerr '54, Big Ten basketball's Most Valuable Player in 1953-54, became the "voice of the Chicago Bulls" after a professional career as a player and coach.

Volleyball superstar Mary Eggers '88 was named "Athlete of the Decade" during a 1991-92 celebration marking ten years of women's athletics.

The starters on the 1942-43 basketball team won the nickname the Whiz Kids for their prowess. From left they are Andy Phillip, Ken Menke, Art Mathisen, Jack Smiley, and Gene Vance.

The 1988 Big Ten Player of the Year, Steve Stricker '89, turned professional and joined the PGA Tour after graduating.

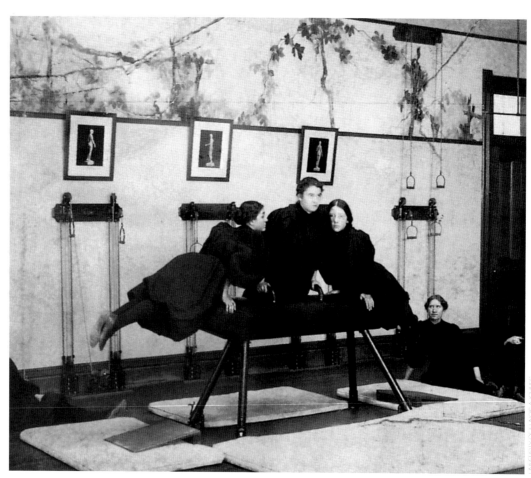

In one of the first physical education classes for
women in 1880, students were required to wear
long skirts and stockings.

Dike Eddleman '49, left, earned
eleven letters in three sports—
basketball, track, and football—and
was an Olympic high jumper. Two of
his University football records still
stand. Teammate Buddy Young '48,
right, set University track and football
records and earned a place in the
professional football Hall of Fame.

All-American catcher Darrin Fletcher '88, became a professional baseball All-Star, playing with the Montreal Expos.

Runner Marianne Dickerson '83 was 1983 Illini female Athlete of the Year.

Playing for the Cleveland Indians, shortstop Lou Boudreau '40, was the best hitter in the American League in 1944, earning the "Flying Frenchman" a spot in the baseball Hall of Fame.

The Civil Engineering Society baseball team prevailed as champions of the 1894 intramural season.

In 1958, this cheerleader carried on a tradition dating from the 1890s, when the Illini had some of the first collegiate cheerleaders in the country.

Gymnastics, 1951.

Women's basketball, 1975.

Illini athlete Don Laz '52, pole vaulted at the 1952 Helsinki Olympics.

An Illini letter winner in track and football, Bobby Mitchell '58 (#22) had a
Hall of Fame career on the professional gridiron and then moved off the field
to serve as assistant general manager of the Washington Redskins.

Ray Nitschke '58,
earned his place in
the football Hall
of Fame playing
for the Green Bay
Packers.

Football #50 was retired after Dick Butkas '65, center,
became a stand-out Chicago Bear and member of the
professional football Hall of Fame.

Tonja Buford '95, topped her 1992 NCAA championship in 400-meter hurdles by making the Olympic team the same year.

Harold "Red" Grange '26, was dubbed the "Galloping Ghost" for his prowess on the gridiron. He led the Fighting Illini through the 1924 and 1925 seasons before launching his professional career with the Chicago Bears. He scored four touchdowns against Michigan in the first quarter of the inaugural game at Memorial Stadium in 1924.

The Marching Illini showed off its first football game formations in 1920, earning the reputation of being "the greatest college band in the world."

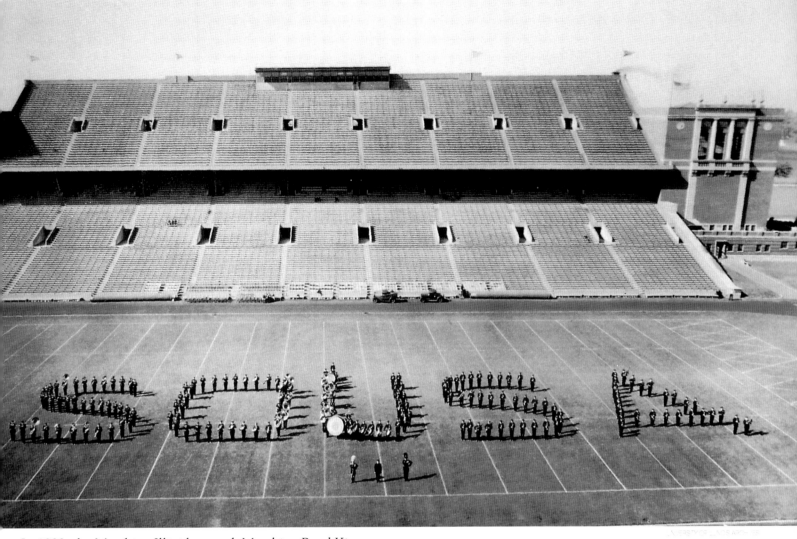

In 1923, the Marching Illini honored Marching Band King
John Philip Sousa, who once served as the band's guest conductor.

Olympic wheelchair racer
Sharon Rahn Hedrick BS '80,
MS '82 captured a gold medal
at the 1988 Olympics in Seoul,
Korea. At the Los Angeles
games in 1984 and in Seoul,
she set world records in the
women's 800-meter event.

Football Coach
Robert Zuppke led his
football teams to four
national and seven
Big Ten championships
between 1914 and
1928. He was quoted
as saying, "Nobody
but a dead man leaves
the field."

Though archery was a women's sport in the late 1920s, critics found the athletes' knee-length skirts to be immodest and decidedly unladylike.

Big Ten wrestling, 1991.

Quarter-miler Herb McKenley '49, set three world records as an Illini and captured a 1952 Olympic gold medal for his native Jamaica.

Celena Mondie-Milner '91, achieved All-America and All-Conference honors more than three dozen times.

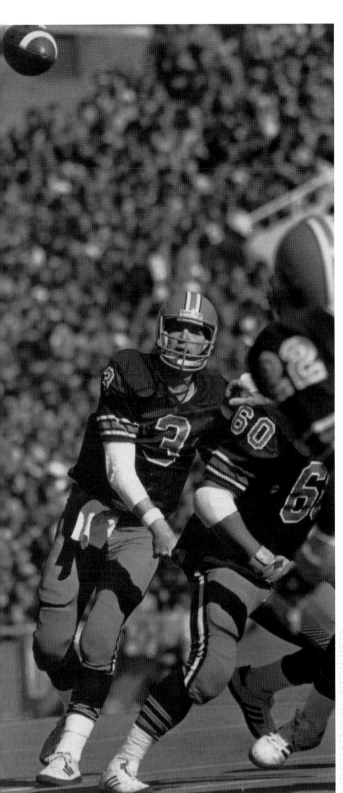

Quarterback Tony Eason '83, had a throwing arm that earned him two record-breaking seasons at Illinois.

George "G" Huff 1892, spent his career at the University as coach for several teams, athletics director and director of the School of Physical Education, where he established the first four-year professional course of study in physical education. He was especially successful in baseball, bringing home eleven championships.

Intramural Riding Club, 1930.

Famous Alumni

Join a reunion of famous alumni, including Roger Ebert, Lynn Martin, and Red Grange. Meet the president of the Philippines, the inventor of the microchip, and the mother of the soap opera.

Chicago's Navy Pier! Walking onto it in early 1960, I began an exciting and important period of my life. Having to work to pay tuition left me no choice but to remain in Chicago. Back then, Navy Pier served as a branch of the University of Illinois at Urbana-Champaign.

Pier folks were a special breed. We were survivors. We endured lake water pouring into classrooms, claustrophobia-inducing narrow hallways, and sprints from the armory to the main building in frigid lakefront weather. Despite the physical surroundings, our professors maintained a learning environment, and we students were grateful for this opportunity of a lifetime.

Two years later, I transferred to the University's Urbana campus. My time was marked by the construction of Assembly Hall, the assassination of JFK, and a flood of wonderful experiences new to a young man who had never before lived away from home. I got to know my slide rule well and was thrilled at the results of my laboratory experiments. I had plenty of time to socialize and philosophize during long walks from Garner Men's Residence Hall to engineering classes. I sometimes arrived tired; my roommate and I stayed up late, occasionally until sunrise, playing chess as if we were in a life-or-death struggle. Memories of the Quad, the Union, games in Huff Gym, and dormitory food are still vivid.

Roger Plummer

I launched my career in 1964 as a management trainee at Illinois Bell. I was ready. My intellectual and personal growth at the University had prepared me not only for the world of work, but also for lifelong learning.

My career with the Bell System, later called Ameritech, was, by most measures, a very successful one. I rose quickly in the ranks of management, mastering operations, sales, and marketing in addition to engineering. In 1981 when I became an officer and vice president of Illinois Bell, I began to reflect on how important the University has been to my professional success. Those days at the Pier and in Urbana came into sharp focus, reinforcing their value.

The University really is a launching pad for successful lives. This fact has been underscored for me through my involvement in organizations such as the Alumni Association, University Foundation, and Colleges of Engineering and Commerce. It was after I achieved professional and personal success that I pledged to give something back to my alma mater, to balance the scales in some small way by working with the University. As president of the Alumni Association, I have the pleasure of meeting other people whose lives were forever bettered by their attendance at the University of Illinois.

Soon my son, Adam, will join the ranks of proud and loyal Illini alumni. There was never a question about where he would further his education. I know that Illinois has started him on the path to personal and professional fulfillment.

Roger Plummer '64

Before retiring as President and CEO of Ameritech's Custom Business Services unit, Roger Plummer '64, was Vice President of Operations at Illinois Bell. He now heads his own firm, Plummer & Associates Consulting.

Mr. Plummer assumed the presidency of the University Alumni Association in May 1995 after serving as vice president for two years. He is the first black president of the 120,000-member organization. Mr. Plummer also serves on the boards of the University of Illinois Foundation, DePaul University, the College of Commerce Advisory Council, WTTW, the public television station in Chicago, and the Executive Council of the International Engineering Consortium.

150

Lorado Taft 1879, ML 1880, with model and sculpture of Christopher Columbus, dedicated in Washington, D.C., in 1912.

George Crumb, M.Music '52, Pulitzer Prize-winning composer.

James "Scotty" Reston '32, left, served as a reporter, columnist, and Washington bureau chief at *The New York Times* and earned two Pulitzer Prizes for national reporting.

Walter Burley Griffin 1899, won a competition to design Australia's capital city, Canberra.

Illini football legend Harold "Red" Grange '26, put professional football in the spotlight as the star of the Chicago Bears. He was a movie actor during the off season.

Chemist Mildred Rebstock *AM '43, PhD '45*, helped develop chloromycetin, the first of the antibiotic wonder drugs to be synthesized in a laboratory. First produced in 1949, chloromycetin was used to treat typhoid, typhus, Rocky Mountain spotted fever and pneumonia.

Jill Wine Banks '64, the only female prosecutor in the Watergate case, later became deputy attorney general of Illinois and chief executive officer of the American Bar Association.

Charlotte Herman Kerr '40, MD '48, internationally known gynecologist and past president of the American Medical Women's Association.

Retired Brigadier General Wilma Vaught '52, helped pioneer the roles of women in the U.S. Air Force and spearheaded a memorial to women in military service begun in 1995.

Newspaper publisher Helene Foellinger '32, began her career as woman's editor at *The Dailly Illini*.

Arnold O. Beckman '22, MS '23, and his wife, Mabel, both at left, donated $40 million to the University for the building of an inter-disciplinary intelligence research center, the Beckman Institute for Advanced Science and Technology. Beckman founded Beckman Instruments with his invention of the pH meter. He was inducted into the National Inventors Hall of Fame in 1987. Sculptor Peter Fagan stands at right.

Herman Krannert '12, far right, founder of Inland Container Corporation, and his wife, Ellnora, shared their wealth with the University by funding the Krannert Art Museum in 1961 and the Krannert Center for the Performing Arts in 1969. Here, they examine a model of the Krannert Center with architect Max Abramovitz '29, far left, and University President David Henry, second from left.

Charles Luckman '31, young president of Lever Brothers, shows off his company's latest suds discovery in 1947. Luckman later made his mark as the architect of Madison Square Garden, the Johnson Space Center and many other structures.

General Fidel Ramos MS '51, President of the Philippines.

In the 1930s, Wallace Carothers MS '21, PhD '24, discovered nylon, the first synthetic fiber, and helped develop neoprene, the first commercially produced, general purpose synthetic rubber.

Jack Kilby '47, inventor of the microchip.

An actor on campus, William Maxwell '30, made his living as a novelist, short story writer, and editor of *The New Yorker* magazine.

Alumnus Steven Nagel '69, back row far left, and former graduate student
Bonnie Dunbar rocketed into space aboard the 1985 Challenger space
shuttle mission. Nagel piloted the mission.

Collett Woolman '12, founder
of Delta Air Lines.

Jerry Hadley M.*Music* '77,
leading operatic tenor.

As an independent candidate, John B. Anderson
'42, JD '46, offered voters a third choice in the
1980 presidential election.

Gene Shalit '49,
funnyman book
and movie
reviewer.

Jean Driscoll '91, MS '93, raced to victory in the Boston
Marathon a record six times, making her the world
marathon champion in her sport.

Nobel laureate Edwin Krebs '40 laid the foundations of human knowledge of the basic principles of cell regulation, including immune responses and cell growth.

James Mann 1876, represented Illinois as a Republican congressman and House minority leader.

Urbana native Roger Ebert '64, was editor of *The Daily Illini* during his senior year and went on to become a Pulitzer Prize-winning film critic at the *Chicago Sun-Times*. Here, he poses in the former Princess Theater in Urbana, where his lifelong love of films was sparked.

"Hello Mudder," a comic song about summer camp, propelled Allan Sherman '45 to fame after an eighteen-year entertainment career that included his creation of the TV hit "I've Got a Secret."

Irna Phillips '23, created more than twenty radio and television soap operas, including the original ones.

162

Athlete-turned-businessman Jerry Colangelo '62 is general manager and part-owner of the Phoenix Suns professional basketball team, and chief executive officer and part-owner of the Arizona Diamondbacks major league baseball expansion team.

Illini basketball star Mannie Jackson '60, became Senior Vice President of corporate marketing at Honeywell Inc. and owner of the Harlem Globetrotters.

Nick Anderson '90, rose to fame in professional basketball as the member of the Orlando Magic who challenged the talents of the Chicago Bulls' Michael Jordan on the court.

Donna Mills '59, actress.

Mission Impossible actress Barbara Bain '52, was known as Mildred Fogel when she was crowned Queen of the 1950 Homecoming.

Alumni Neal Doughty '69, far left, Alan Gratzer '70, center, and Gregg Philbin '69 (not shown here), along with two others, started the popular rock group REO Speedwagon during their college days, practicing in the Illinois Street Residence Halls.

Andrea Evans '79, soap opera star.

Football letterman Peter Palmer '54, second from right, was Broadway's *L'il Abner* in 1956.

Arte Johnson '49, cracked up television viewers of *Rowan and Martin's Laugh-In* and has continued acting on the big screen.

Nick Holonyak Jr. '50, MS '51, PhD '54, invented the visible semiconductor diode laser. In addition to uses in displays, medicine, and optical communications, it is the principal component in compact disc players.

John Welch Jr. MS '59, PhD '61, Chairman and Chief Executive Officer of General Electric Company.

Avery Brundage '09, competed in the 1912 Olympic pentathlon and served for two decades as president of the International Olympic Committee.

Jeff George '91 (#11), left Illinois in 1990 to become a quarterback for the
Indianapolis Colts. A first-round draft choice, he signed for a record $15 million.

Claude "Buddy"
Young '48 set Illini
records in track and
football, was inducted
into the professional
football Hall of Fame
and served as Special
Assistant to the
Commissioner of the
National Football
League.

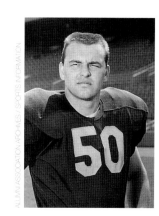

Number 50 was retired
in honor of Dick
Butkas '65, who went
on to play for the
Chicago Bears.

Hugh Hefner '49, founder of
Playboy Enterprises.

Ben Abruzzo '52, second from left, made the first-ever successful
crossings of the Atlantic and Pacific Oceans in a balloon. Here, he
and his teammates gathered with their wives to celebrate their
1978 Atlantic accomplishment.

Donald Johanson '66,
an anthropologist,
discovered
"Lucy," the
oldest and most
complete fossil
skeleton of a
prehuman
ancestor.

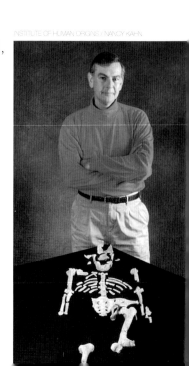

J. Robert Schrieffer MS '54, *PhD '57*, accepted the National
Medal of Science from President Ronald Reagan in 1984.
The federal government's highest scientific honor recognized
Schrieffer's research in condensed matter physics. In 1972,
Schrieffer shared the Nobel Prize in physics with University
Professor John Bardeen and University researcher Leon Cooper
for developing the theory of superconductivity.

Thomas Murphy
'38, retired
chairman of
General Motors
Corporation.

Breakfast with "Budge," *Christian Science Monitor* Washington bureau chief Godfrey Sperling Jr. '37, far left, provided the press corps a chance to meet informally with the day's newsmakers, such as President Gerald Ford in 1976.

Temple Hoyne Buell '16, designed the first modern shopping mall and left money to the University for a new architecture building.

President Ronald Reagan's Press Secretary, James Brady '62, monitored several news broadcasts by watching a wall of television sets in 1981. Brady was permanently disabled in 1981 when he was struck by a bullet intended for the president. He now lobbies for gun control measures such as the Brady Bill, passed in 1993.

Astronaut Dale Gardner '70, retrieved a wayward $35 million communications satellite from space during a 1984 Discovery shuttle mission.

Joseph Tanner '73, astronaut.

As founder of the Catholic Worker Movement, Dorothy Day '18 attended a church service for farm workers with United Farm Workers union leader Cesar Chavez and Coretta Scott King in 1973.

Representing Illinois for a decade, Republican Lynn Martin '60, was the first freshman on the House Budget Committee. She went on to become Secretary of Labor under President George Bush.

Frederick Marx '77, edited and produced the 1994 award-winning documentary, *Hoop Dreams*.

Rosalyn Yalow MS '42, *PhD '45*, earned a Nobel Prize in medicine in 1977 for her development of radioimmunoassay, the use of radioactive isotopes as tracers to measure minute substances in the body.

To thy happy children of the future,
those of the past send greetings.

Her children arise up
and call her blessed.

ACKNOWLEDGMENTS

The success of a book like this one relies on the coordinated efforts of many individuals. Our thanks go to the following people for their expertise and assistance: in particular, the staff of the University of Illinois Archives, especially Robert Chapel; and Ruth Weinard, Associate Director Communications, University of Illinois Alumni Association; as well as Julie Dalpiaz, Publications Coordinator, Division of Intercollegiate Athletics; Donald Dodds, Urbana Director, University of Illinois Alumni Association; John Fundator, Communications Associate, University of Illinois Foundation; Nancy Gilmore, Managing Editor, *Illinois Quarterly*; Pamela Hohn, Assistant to the Associate Chancellor for Public Affairs, Office of Public Affairs; Judith Jones, Coordinator for External Relations, Beckman Institute for Advanced Science and Technology; Robin Kaler, Visiting Editorial Associate, Office of the Chancellor; Louis Liay, Executive Director, University of Illinois Alumni Association; Rebecca McBride, Assistant Director for Marketing, Krannert Center for the Performing Arts; John Melchi, Public Information Officer, National Center for Supercomputing Applications; Mike Pearson, Sports Information Director, Division of Intercollegiate Athletics; Phyllis J. Piano, Manager of Public Relations Programs, General Electric Company; Mary Targonski, A.V. Technician, DuPont External Affairs; Alexis Tate, Associate Director, University Office of Public Affairs; and the entire the staff of the University of Illinois Alumni Association.

Special thanks to the following for writing introductory essays: University President James Stukel; Chancellor Michael Aiken; Cesar Pelli; John Cribbet, Chancellor Emeritus; Jennifer Sherlock; Daniel Perrino; Dennis Swanson; and Roger Plummer.

Editor/Director of Research: Christine Netznik
Project Manager/Art Director: Evelyn C. Shapiro
Designer: Carlton Bruett
Director of Photography: Daniel Leasure
Editorial Consultant/Historian: Ruth Weinard
Research Assistant: Mabel C. Thurmon
Marketing Director: Melissa Yoars

This book has been typeset in Goudy for text and Bauer Bodoni for display type. Page layouts were created by Carlton Bruett, Daniel Leasure, and Evelyn C. Shapiro.

The illustrations were made by All Systems Color in Miamisburg, Ohio, from 175-line screen separations and halftones. Walsworth Publishing in Marceline, Missouri, printed the pages using two- and five-color offset lithography on sheetfed acid-free, 100-pound Signature Dull paper. The jacket has been printed in four colors with a matte lamination. The sheets were smyth sewn in sixteen-page signatures and cased in ICG Kennett cloth.